SELF-REGULATION

A Guide to Avoiding Natural Consequences

Justin Boynton

Self-Regulation

A Guide to Avoiding Natural Consequences

Copyright 2025, **Justin M. Boynton**

Published by Justin Boynton
ISBN: 979-8-9892234-5-9
For information, contact:
voiceoftheforgottenusa@gmail.com
Printed in the United States of America

Table of Contents

PART ONE: THE PROBLEM

THE DAILY CROSSROADS

You made a decision this morning. Maybe several. And you didn't question a single one of them.

Your alarm went off. You hit snooze. Someone needed help; you scrolled past. Money came in; you kept it. Each choice felt automatic.

But what if none of those thoughts were truly yours?

What if the voice telling you "just five more minutes," "you've earned this," or "they'll be fine without you" isn't you at all? What if every decision you think you're making freely is actually being made for you by something you can't see?

These aren't philosophical questions. This is your daily reality. And until you recognize it, you'll keep making the same contaminated choices, suffering the same consequences, and wondering why change seems impossible. To address this, you must understand what self-regulation truly means.

What Is Self-Regulation?

Self-regulation means having the ability to recognize and manage your own thoughts and impulses, rather than simply acting on them automatically. It is not just the control of one's impulses; it is the awareness that guidance is often missing, and the realization that the internal compass, the mechanism that directs right actions, can spin without direction. Self-regulation is the moment you understand that each step must be chosen with care.

But here lies the danger: what feels right to you may lead you further from the truth. What feels right may, in fact, be the very opposite of what you should be doing.

We Are Slaves to Our Thoughts

Most of us operate on autopilot, reacting to whatever thoughts come to mind.

We become reactive to our thoughts, which we think, and, as a result, become slaves to the flesh, unable to self-discipline or self-regulate our actions.

Picture yourself in the morning. Your alarm goes off. Immediately, a thought appears: "Just five more minutes." You don't question it. You don't examine it. You react to it. This is the slavery I'm talking about. You're not the one choosing; the choice is being made for you.

The Foundation: Your Thoughts Are Not Your Own

Before proceeding, understand this: your thoughts, meaning the ideas, impulses, and reactions that arise in your mind each day, are not your own.

There is an influence of evil contaminating your thoughts. This is why you forget things. This is why you injure yourself. This is why car accidents occur. This is why people kill other people. This is why there are wars. This is why there are divorces. This is why friendships don't last a lifetime. This is why there are so many denominations of churches. This is why you hoard money. This is why you don't serve others. This is why there are orphan children. This is why there is homelessness.

I t is darkness that contaminates the mind and destroys.

B ut what you can't see, hear, feel, or touch is the deception. The mind is deceived into believing these things are normal or even good. Deceit is their greatest weapon.

And it fills every mind that walks this planet. Christians believe they are free from the deceit, and that belief itself is the deception. You must recognize your mind is contaminated, or you will be a slave to it.

The Question Every Believer Must Ask

Why has everyone sinned?

If you call yourself a believer and you follow God, have you ever truly wrestled with this question? Where does this sin come from? Why have you sinned? Why are we all sinners?

This is the deception at work in your mind. You cannot even see where it comes from. So, let me ask you directly: Where does sin originate? Is it some magical outside force that occasionally sweeps by you and makes you do something you don't want to do?

No. It's your mind, contaminated by a darkness you cannot see.

"For we are not fighting against flesh-and-blood enemies, but against evil rulers and authorities of the unseen world,

against mighty powers in this dark world." (Ephesians 6:12, NLT)

However, you can definitely hear it if you pay attention. The influences of hate, pride, fear, lust, selfishness, and greed are constantly whispering in your mind. All you have to do is become conscious of it!

Learning to Listen to the Whispers

Listen! Listen to what they say. Listen to what they whisper. This is the feeling you have in the flesh. The whisper is not an audible voice, but a feeling within you.

Have you felt fear? What does that whisper feel like? Where do you feel it? How does it affect you? Have you ever felt you wanted something? Desired something of this world? A job, a new promotion, a new house, a new car? That's lust. Have you ever wanted to hold onto money instead of giving it away? Put it into savings for a rainy day? That's greed. Have you ever not wanted to share something of yours? That's selfishness. Have you ever criticized someone? That's hate.

Let me give you an example. You're in line at the grocery store. The person in front of you is taking forever, fumbling with coupons, and asking the cashier questions. You feel irritation rising. There it is, the whisper of hate. "Why can't they be more prepared?" whispers hate. "They're so inconsiderate," whispers selfishness.

That thought feels justified, doesn't it? It feels like a natural response to an annoying situation. But that's the deception. That irritation, that judgment, it's not born of love. It's hate bubbling up to the surface. A contaminated program of the flesh has been activated.

Or consider this: you're scrolling through social media and see someone's vacation photos. "Must be nice," you think. "Some people have all the luck." That small seed of resentment is born from hate.

But these whispers don't just come from within; they are amplified by the world around us, especially through what we see and hear every day.

TV, Movies, Social Media: The Mediums of Darkness

If I am filled with darkness, if the flesh is contaminated, how do I feed the darkness within? It has an appetite. It is hungry. And it needs to be fed.

It is said that the eyes are the window to the soul. And how true this is! How does darkness contaminate the spirit? Through what passes before your eyes.

Darkness is blasted into your mind at nearly every moment possible.

Even in the most simplistic and wholehearted of shows or movies, you will find darkness being transmitted to you. Betrayal, fear, and rejection form the foundation of nearly everything you see.

Acts of murder, assault, and adultery appear so frequently that they become normal in your mind. This is hate being transmitted directly to your spirit, and you've become so accustomed to it that you can't even see it anymore.

The screen has become your teacher. It shows you what to want, what to fear, and what to accept as normal. It whispers that betrayal is expected, violence is entertaining, lust is natural, and greed is wise.

And you sit before it willingly. You pay for the privilege. You arrange your schedule around it. You defend your favorite shows, your must-watch series, your comfort content.

But what comfort does darkness bring?

What rest comes from feeding the contamination within?

The Greatest Disaster You Cannot See

This place, this temporary home, has experienced the greatest disaster that has ever happened to it, and you're not aware of it. The deception is so great in our minds that you cannot even see the greatest disaster: darkness entering what was once light.

"Then the Lord God said, 'Look, the human beings have become like us, knowing both good and evil.'" (Genesis 3:22, NLT)

This darkness, this evil, its greatest weapon is deception of the mind. It deceives you into believing what you know is correct and right, even though it is wrong. This is the great deception of the mind: to make you believe you know what is right.

"What sorrow for those who say that evil is good and good is evil, that dark is light and light is dark, that bitter is sweet and sweet is bitter." (Isaiah 5:20, NLT)

PART TWO: WHY WE NEED CHECKLISTS

HOW INDUSTRIES LEARNED to Work with the Mind

If our minds were uncorrupted, there would be no need for pilots to use checklists, for governments to create procedures, or for corporations to write policies. We would all know what is correct, and we would all know how to function with the universal good that was within us. We would know what was right, and we would just automatically do it. We wouldn't need a book or a manual to tell us.

But this is not the world that we live in. This is not the creation we inhabit.

The Airline Industry's Solution

The airline industry is one profession that has mastered this practice best. Although they have never been aware of why pilots' minds are contaminated, they have definitely done their best to mitigate the natural consequences of the contamination.

Before an airplane even pushes away from the gate, the pilots have completed a checklist. This checklist contains approximately 250 items that they must review before they're even allowed to push away from the gate. Imagine that! A detailed list of 250 items that they must verify before the plane even moves.

And before they take flight, there are approximately 50 more items they must check.

These checklists have been built over decades through accidents and errors. Because of the contamination of the mind, people have died. So the industry developed a way to work with a contaminated mind.

Think about what this means. The airline industry, through tragic experience, learned that you cannot trust a human mind, even a highly trained, professional pilot's mind, to remember everything. The mind forgets. The mind overlooks. The mind misses.

So they created external systems to compensate for internal failure. They didn't try to make perfect pilots. They acknowledged imperfect minds and built safeguards around them.

This is what one very important industry has done on its own to work with a mind that forgets, that can't remember, that overlooks important things, professional minds that have failed and caused the deaths of thousands.

W hy does the mind fail?

C orporate Policy Manuals Reveal the Problem
If you've ever worked for the government, a company, or a corporation, you will know they have standard operating procedures, a policy manual on what you should do and how you should do it. Why are these even necessary?

It is because each individual who comes under the umbrella of a corporation has their own belief on what is correct or what is right. This individual belief is not something that happens randomly. It is because each one of us is individually influenced by the darkness that contaminates our minds.

But if you know what is right, why does your workplace have a policy manual to tell you what is right? If you know what you're doing, why are there checklists to tell you what to do?

Is their right better than your right? Is your truth better than others' truth? Nobody knows. But you think you know, and they think they know. How can you, who think you are right, follow someone else's rules? Why couldn't you just follow your own internal guidance system? Your belief system? Why are there laws to keep you within certain boundaries?

Everyone thinks they are right, yet they are blind to how they are under others' guidance. You leave the house, and you fall under the government's rules of conduct. You enter a grocery store and are subject to their rules for how to behave within their establishment. You go to work and are subject to the employer's rules. How can you be right and yet need guidance at every step?

C an a mind that is evil produce a good thought?

O ur Checklist for Life
The best guide or checklist we have available has been in use for thousands of years. All other things have been

contaminated by man. Everything ever written, every guide, every book has the influence of evil working through it. "For you who are evil" is what the holiest one to ever walk the Earth once said about mankind.

The best checklist we have ever been given is a compilation of 66 books. These books were assembled to show us what is correct in a world that is incorrect, to guide us on the right path and help us avoid the consequences of evil.

Because our minds are contaminated, we can never know what is correct on our own. But the 66 books are the absolute closest thing to living in truth that we have.

Do you need to know all 66 books and what they say in order to avoid the consequences of this life? No. There are some key books and some key guidance that help you self-regulate, because you must know some basic truths in order to choose the road with the least amount of natural consequences.

PART THREE: LEARNING DISCIPLINE

HOW WE LEARN (OR DON'T Learn) Self-Regulation

Picture a young child walking through the store with their parents. They see something they want, and they take it and put it in their pocket. What would their parents do?

Greed influenced that child, and they took what they wanted. Even the youngest of children are influenced by the darkness. A child who doesn't want to share a toy, or who screams and yells because they have to do something they don't want to do, are being influenced.

This young child hopefully receives guidance and discipline when they're young. But what happens to this child when they're older? When there are no parents around to guide or discipline?

We are left to the consequences of this world to punish us. And the consequences are not kind to us. This world is cruel. It will reject us, betray us, abuse us, abandon us, and use us. These are just a couple of the many natural consequences we can incur if we don't self-regulate.

Discipline Versus Punishment

We must understand that discipline comes from love and that punishment comes from hate.

Most of us were punished as children, and so we avoid correction. Punishment is painful, it is harsh, and there is no kindness in it. Punishment is hurtful and can be downright miserable. As adults, we associate consequences or correction with punishment, a painful action designed to crush our spirits.

And this is what the world does to us as adults. It can be crushing and devastating.

There are those who learn to manipulate this world, create their own rules, and use other human beings as tools for their own enjoyment, satisfaction, and pleasure. This is the manifestation of evil, where you exploit your brothers and sisters for your own gain or pleasure. This is what the influence, the contamination, of evil has done to the creation. We now just use one another for what we need or want.

Becoming Part of the World to Survive It

So, as adults, this world punishes us. That's what these consequences are. So what do you do? You learn to operate in this world to avoid the punishment of it.

But by doing that, you become part of the world. You assimilate with the world around you so it doesn't reject you, criticize you, so it doesn't spit you out and leave you on the sidewalk poor and homeless.

You must allow pride to work within you; otherwise, you will not have a chance at worldly success. You must allow hate to function through you, or how else will you take what you need from others? You must allow greed to be influential so you can negotiate a better price on everything, a better wage, and pocket as much as possible.

Even the most faithful negotiate a better price for themselves. Where does this come from? Greed and its cousin, selfishness.

Pride and deceit make you think you're exempt from the suffering and the consequences of this world. Christians who don't believe they have a demon of greed within them go out and negotiate better prices on everything, all the while knowing all things belong to Him. If the man believes his lawn tractor is worth $2,000, then why do you try to get it for $1,800? To take from another? Or are you being responsible with God's resources?

Both the lawn tractor and the money are God's, so how are you protecting His interests by giving less? Are we not called to be givers? Don't be fooled by the demons of deceit. You are contaminated with greed. Everyone is, and no one is exempt.

Give to the creation what belongs to the creation and give to God what belongs to God. Do not become a part of this world, or you will be lost to it. Heaven is not full of greedy people. It is filled with givers.

A Simple Example: Dental Care

This too is self-regulation: choosing what is good when influenced by what is not. Let's take a look at everyone's favorite subject, dental care.

Laziness, which is born of hate, will tell you not to floss or brush your teeth. What are the consequences of listening to that thought? Soon cavities will form, and if they are ignored, the roots will become infected, leading to an abscessed tooth. If left untreated, the tooth will eventually need to be pulled.

As a child, you were taught to brush your teeth. That self-regulation, that discipline, should carry through into your adult life. You have now chosen to brush your teeth and floss your teeth so many times in your life that this good habit becomes normal. You may not even remember when you had to be told to brush your teeth.

This is a simple illustration of self-regulation: choosing to do good before you suffer the consequences of bad.

So, your parents taught you to brush your teeth, and they constantly reminded you and even supervised you when you were young.

Were you ever taught about talking about someone when they're not present? Chances are, almost no one was taught that. So how would you know it was wrong and the consequences that come from it?

I t's in the manual of life.

PART FOUR: FIVE PRINCIPAL INFECTIONS

THESE ARE THE FIVE principal infections of the flesh. These are the things that contaminate your mind in thousands of different ways. There are only five, but when they start combining with things of this world and different actions throughout your day, they multiply into a mind that can't think correctly.

Why do you think they offer so many different types of cereal, different types of cars, and different styles of clothing? All of this contamination has created a multitude of different personalities and characteristics, prompting people to exploit them for financial gain. These are not just likes or personal tastes. All of this is offered because of one thing: darkness.

People do not change cars frequently or clothes frequently because they walk in the love of the spirit. It is because hate tells you that you are not good enough, or because pride tells you that you should have a newer, better car. All of these whispers, all of these voices that we hear, affect how we live every second of every day.

1. HATE

Are you exempt from hate? It manifests itself in so many ways you're unaware of it.

Here is something that hate does, and I know you've done it, so you can become aware that hate infects your life: *talking about someone when they are not present.*

"What?" you say. "That's not hate!"

This is one of the most subtle things that hate does. It is so common that you will not even recognize it as hate.

The Spiritual Mechanics of Gossip

What happens when you talk about someone who isn't present?

We all connect through the spirit first; you must understand this. This is why you might feel comfortable around some people and uncomfortable around others. It is what they carry in the spirit. It is the connection you make with them.

So when you talk about someone, you're not connecting with them in the spirit. If you truly wanted to know and cared about the person, you would talk to them. Talking about them when they're not around is gossip. Gossip is born of hate.

What happens spiritually when I talk about someone else? I share that hate with someone, and now that someone knows I'm a sharer of hate. So what does someone who receives hate do with it? They share it! They share the hate that I shared, and so hate gets spread around the world.

Will they talk about me? Why wouldn't they talk about me? My sharing of hate allows them to share hate as well. So gossip spreads like a wildfire, and you will pay the price for what you have shared. In this, you will reap what you sow.

What the Manual Says About Gossip

Warnings Against Gossip:

- "Do not go about spreading slander among your people." (Leviticus 19:16)
- "A gossip betrays a confidence, but a trustworthy person keeps a secret." (Proverbs 11:13)
- "Without wood a fire goes out; without a gossip a quarrel dies down." (Proverbs 26:20)
- "The words of a gossip are like choice morsels; they go down to the inmost parts." (Proverbs 18:8)
- "They are gossips, slanderers, God-haters..." (Romans 1:29–30)

Consequences of Gossip:

- "A perverse person stirs up conflict, and a gossip separates close friends." (Proverbs 16:28)
- "He who goes about as a slanderer reveals secrets, therefore do not associate with a gossip." (Proverbs 20:19)
- "For lack of wood the fire goes out, and where there is no whisperer, contention quiets down." (Proverbs 26:20)
- "You will give an account on the day of judgment for every careless word you have spoken." (Matthew 12:36)

Checklist to Combat Gossip:

☐ "Keep your tongue from evil and your lips from telling lies." (Psalm 34:13)

☐ "Let no corrupting talk come out of your mouths, but only such as is good for building up, that it may give grace to those who hear." (Ephesians 4:29)

☐ "Brothers and sisters, do not slander one another." (James 4:11)

☐ "If anyone thinks he is religious and does not bridle his tongue but deceives his heart, this person's religion is worthless." (James 1:26)

☐ "In everything, set an example by doing what is good. In your teaching show integrity, seriousness, and soundness of speech." (Titus 2:7 8)

That is exactly how you would know it was wrong and the consequences that come with it. There is a checklist, a policy manual, and standard operating procedures for life on Earth. But you must know them before you can follow them, and you must follow them to avoid the cruel consequences of this world.

If you have a standard operating policy at your place of employment and you operate outside of it, and it causes trouble, are you free of any consequences? Most employers will hold you accountable if you operate outside of their policy and something bad happens. The same is true with life. If you operate outside of the manual you were given, if you don't self-regulate, you will suffer the cruel consequences of this world.

Criticism Is Hate

Criticizing another human being or what they've done is born of hate.

"Look at what they did." "They can't do anything right." "Did you hear what this person did?" "You didn't do this right."

Any criticizing or judgment of another does not come from love. It is born purely of hate.

If you've ever attended church for a number of years, you will see hate. Why is that? Why do people leave some churches and change to other churches? Is God not in the church?

Is there a better God in a different church? Is God's presence felt differently in another church? Maybe God loves another church more than the church you were in?

It is all hate that destroys, because we are all contaminated. Every single person is contaminated, even the people within the church. This is the creation. This is the truth.

Recognize hate in your life! If you deny it, you give it strength and you give it power. Hate works in the absence of recognition.

The Physical Manifestation of Hate

Hate is like thick, sticky tar. Once it seeps in, it breeds laziness and lethargy. Hate keeps you from cleaning the house, scheduling the health checkup, or fixing a leaky roof until the damage becomes even worse. Where there is laziness, there is hate. God gives you a home and a place to stay, but if you let garbage pile up and neglect what you have been given, you show disregard for that gift. Hate destroys God's blessings through laziness. Be very careful with this because it is incredibly destructive.

What the Manual Says About Hate

Warnings Against Hate:

- "The one who hates his brother is in the darkness and walks in the darkness." (1 John 2:11)
- "Anyone who claims to love God yet hates a brother or sister is a liar." (1 John 4:20)
- "Everyone who hates his brother is a murderer, and you know that no murderer has eternal life abiding in him." (1 John 3:15)
- "You have heard that it was said, 'Love your neighbor and hate your enemy.' But I tell you, love your enemies and pray for those who persecute you." (Matthew 5:43 44)

Consequences of Hate:

- "Hatred stirs up conflict, but love covers over all wrongs." (Proverbs 10:12)
- "Because of the increase of wickedness, the love of most will grow cold." (Matthew 24:12)
- "He who conceals hatred has lying lips, and whoever spreads slander is a fool." (Proverbs 10:18)
- "The way of the wicked is like deep darkness; they do not know what makes them stumble." (Proverbs 4:19)

C hecklist to Combat Hate:

☐ "Do not repay anyone evil for evil... If your enemy is hungry, feed him; if he is thirsty, give him something to drink." (Romans 12:17, 20)

☐ "Love your enemies, do good to them, and lend to them without expecting to get anything back." (Luke 6:35)

☐ "Let all bitterness and wrath and anger and clamor and slander be put away from you, along with all malice." (Ephesians 4:31)

☐ "Above all, love each other deeply, because love covers over a multitude of sins." (1 Peter 4:8)

☐ "Do not be overcome by evil, but overcome evil with good." (Romans 12:21)

2. FEAR

This one is easier to recognize, but still, people walk around blinded.

Fear is a demon. Did you know that? It is what cripples you, keeps you from walking in faith. It's a powerful tool for greed. This is why people hoard money; greed and fear are an incredible combination.

What about fear and selfishness combined? Now we're really talking about a powerful couple.

How Fear Powers Other Infections

Don't think any of these work independently of the other. Almost all demons need fear for strength, power, and influence. Hate cannot influence without fear. If you do not have a fear of hate, then hate cannot cripple you and hide your light.

This is why Christians serve Christians. This is why pastors preach to the saved. This is why the saved serve the church, because the demon of fear influences them.

Fear of hate and fear of the world keep Christians behind closed doors with one another. Fear is an incredibly powerful tool of the darkness. It paralyzes nearly every person.

Fear of Hate: The Silent Paralysis

Peter walked with Jesus. He saw the miracles, the dead raised, the blind given sight. He heard the teachings firsthand. He was so convinced of his loyalty that he declared: **"Even if all fall away on account of you, I never will... Even if I have to die with you, I will never disown you."** (Matthew 26:33, 35)

And when the moment came, surrounded by those who wanted Jesus dead, Peter denied Him. Three times. Just as Jesus predicted.

You know why someone who had seen Jesus's miracles, who had seen people raised from the dead, who had seen life breathed into dead bodies - this man who followed Jesus and said he would die with Jesus, who was so passionate about Jesus's love, His miracles, and His work and the forgiveness - denied Him? Why would he deny Christ not once but three times?

Fear of hate. Peter was surrounded by hate and people who wanted to kill. The atmosphere was thick with demons of hate, and fear whispered: "Deny, deny, deny." Run from hate, flee from the darkness that wants to destroy you. Hide from hate.

Hate is a powerful evil force, so powerful that it activated Peter, who was contaminated with fear of hate, and made him deny the Messiah.

"Then Peter remembered the word Jesus had spoken: 'Before the rooster crows, you will disown me three times.' And he went outside and wept bitterly." (Matthew 26:75)

So if Peter, who walked with Jesus, had fear of hate within him, and it was so strong that he denied his friend, his Savior, how do you, who have never seen a miracle performed by Jesus, think you're exempt from the contamination of fear of hate?

The contamination is universal. No one is exempt.

Think about the last time you had an opportunity to speak truth to someone who needed to hear it. Maybe a coworker was making unethical decisions. Maybe a family member was headed down a destructive path. Perhaps you witnessed injustice and had the opportunity to speak out.

What stopped you? Fear. Fear of conflict. Fear of rejection. Fear of being criticized. Fear of guilt. Fear whispered: "Don't do it. They'll judge you. You'll feel bad. Just keep your mouth closed."

And so the light that should have shone remained hidden.

Be aware of this demon and its power over you. The influence of fear can leave you crippled and paralyzed.

Are you conscious of and can you feel the influence of fear in your life?

What the Manual Says About Fear

Warnings Against Fear:

- "Do not be afraid or terrified because of them, for the Lord your God goes with you; he will never leave you nor forsake you." (Deuteronomy 31:6)

- "Say to those with fearful hearts, 'Be strong, do not fear; your God will come.'" (Isaiah 35:4)

- "Do not call conspiracy everything this people calls a conspiracy; do not fear what they fear, and do not dread it." (Isaiah 8:12)

- "Fear of man will prove to be a snare, but whoever trusts in the Lord is kept safe." (Proverbs 29:25)

Consequences of Fear:

- "In cowardly fear they turned back in the day of battle." (Psalm 78:9)

- "But the cowardly, the unbelieving, the vile, the murderers... they will be consigned to the fiery lake of burning sulfur." (Revelation 21:8)

- "Why are you fearful, O you of little faith?" (Matthew 8:26)

C hecklist to Combat Fear:

☐ "The Lord is my light and my salvation, whom shall I fear?" (Psalm 27:1)

☐ "When I am afraid, I put my trust in you." (Psalm 56:3)

☐ "So do not fear, for I am with you; do not be dismayed, for I am your God." (Isaiah 41:10)

☐ "Even though I walk through the darkest valley, I will fear no evil, for you are with me." (Psalm 23:4)

☐ "For God gave us a spirit not of fear but of power and love and self-control." (2 Timothy 1:7) ☐ "There is no fear in love. But perfect love drives out fear." (1 John 4:18)

3. PRIDE

Pride is perhaps the most dangerous infection because it makes you believe you don't have a problem. It's the virus that says you're above the contamination, smarter than the system, exempt from the consequences that destroy everyone else.

Solomon is the perfect example. He once said he never kept anything from himself. Whatever his heart desired, he obtained. According to 1 Kings 11:3, Solomon had 700 wives of royal birth and 300 concubines, totaling 1,000 women.

The passage goes on to say that "his wives turned his heart away" from God. This lack of self-regulation would lead to a dark end in his life. It was ironic, because this was the man who had written extensively about pride and its consequences.

PRIDE AND THE STADIUM

What about football? What about basketball, soccer, hockey, or any sport where teams compete?

These could not exist without pride and hate working together.

God's creation was not designed to be in conflict with one another. The creation was made for serving one another in love, not for pitting people against each other, states against states, or cities against cities.

But pride wants to identify with a conquering team. Pride wants to align itself with strength, with dominance, with winners. Pride feeds on the defeat of others.

And hate? Hate provides the fuel. Hate toward the opposing team. Hate toward the rival city. Hate disguised as "passion," or "loyalty," or "tradition." The contamination is so evident that we teach our young children to compete against one another in organized youth sports. The idea that hate and pride are fun is deeply ingrained in our very existence.

These two demons work together to create an entire industry built on conflict, on competition, on one side crushing the other for entertainment.

T his is how you know you are contaminated.

The Winner and the Loser
What happens to the team that wins?

Pride swells. Pleasure floods in. "We're the best. We're champions. We conquered." The fans celebrate, not in humble gratitude, but in triumphant superiority. They parade through the streets. They mock the losers. They wear their victory like a crown, a crown of pride.

What happens to the team that loses?

Shame enters. Hate rises. Anger at the referees, the coaches, the players who failed. Despair whispers, "We weren't good enough."

Then hate digs deeper: "You aren't good enough."

It's a reminder of that voice they hear constantly. Darkness settles in and stays until the next game, the next season, the next chance to prove superiority. To silence the whisper. To finally feel "I am good enough."

But the pleasure is fleeting. It always is. And the cycle begins again.

So who wins in the end at a sporting event?

S ATAN.

Whether your team wins or loses, darkness wins. Pride or shame. Triumph or despair. Either way, the contamination spreads. Either way, you are further from love.

The winner is enslaved to pride. The loser is enslaved to the whispers of hate. And millions gather to watch it happen, to participate in it, to fund it, to organize their lives around it.

This is not walking in the purpose God has given us. This is not unity in love. This is not serving one another.

Greed? It's there in every ticket sold, every jersey purchased, every bet placed. Pride? Saturating every win, every boast, every claim of superiority. Hate? Woven through every rivalry, every insult hurled at the opposing team. Guilt and shame? They follow every loss, every failure to perform.

This is the outward manifestation of our spiritual decay.

And we call it entertainment.

The Virus That Says "I'm Smart"

Pride is one of the greatest contaminants of the mind. It whispers, "I'm smart." Pride is foolish, yet it convinces itself it's wise. Those who believe its lies take the most senseless actions, thinking themselves superior. Pride blinds you while persuading you that you see more clearly than anyone else.

Consider the manager who refuses to take notes in meetings because he believes he'll remember everything. Three days later, he missed a critical deadline because he forgot. Or the driver who doesn't use GPS because she "knows the way," only to arrive an hour late to an important appointment.

Pride told Solomon he was the exception. Pride whispered that the rules didn't apply to him. Pride said he was strong enough, wise enough, special enough to handle what would destroy other men.

Pride lied. And pride lies to you, too.

Here was the wisest man who ever lived, and yet he could not regulate himself. He possessed all the knowledge, wisdom, and understanding, but he lacked self-regulation.

Knowledge without discipline is useless. Wisdom without action is meaningless. Solomon knew what was right, but he did not do it.

This is the warning for all of us. It doesn't matter how much you know. It doesn't matter how wise you think you are. Without self-regulation, without the discipline to act on what you know, you will fall just as Solomon did.

What the Manual Says About Pride

Warnings Against Pride:
• "When pride comes, then comes disgrace, but with humility comes wisdom." (Proverbs 11:2)

• "Pride goes before destruction, a haughty spirit before a fall." (Proverbs 16:18)

• "The Lord detests all the proud of heart. Be sure of this: They will not go unpunished." (Proverbs 16:5)

• "The arrogance of your heart has deceived you." (Obadiah 1:3)

Consequences of Pride:

• "In his pride the wicked man does not seek him; in all his thoughts there is no room for God." (Psalm 10:4)

• "The pride of your heart has deceived you... though you soar like the eagle and make your nest among the stars, from there I will bring you down, declares the Lord." (Obadiah 1:3 4)

• "The eyes of the arrogant will be humbled and human pride brought low; the Lord alone will be exalted in that day." (Isaiah 2:11)

• "For everyone who exalts himself will be humbled, and he who humbles himself will be exalted." (Luke 14:11)

Checklist to Combat Pride:

☐ "Do nothing out of selfish ambition or vain conceit. Rather, in humility value others above yourselves." (Philippians 2:3)

☐ "Clothe yourselves with humility toward one another, because, 'God opposes the proud but shows favor to the humble.'" (1 Peter 5:5)

☐ "Humble yourselves before the Lord, and he will lift you up." (James 4:10)

☐ "Let the one who boasts boast in the Lord." (1 Corinthians 1:31)

□ "Take my yoke upon you and learn from me, for I am gentle and humble in heart, and you will find rest for your souls." (Matthew 11:29)

4. GREED (and its Cousin, Selfishness)

Do you want that bigger house? Do you want more land? Do you want the newer car? Do you want that new boat? Do you want to have one million dollars in the bank?

Hoarding Money Is an Act of Faithlessness

We call it a savings account. We call it a good investment. But what is it really? It is self-reliance. And this too is a sin.

Jesus said it would be difficult for the rich to enter heaven, and this is very true. But is it because they are rich? What does the money in their bank account have to do with salvation? Many people who claim to be Christians have wealth.

You must understand the influence behind wealth. It is simple: *it is taking*. You must take from the creation to build wealth. This is why it will be nearly impossible for anyone who holds wealth to enter heaven. Heaven is for those who have given, not those who have taken. You will not find any takers in heaven. Each one who is in heaven is willing to give their life for yours. That is the ultimate giver.

So why do we hoard money?

B ecause the mind is contaminated with greed, selfishness, and fear.

If you look around, you will find that saving money is a common practice here. It is not only normal, but people strive their entire life to save as much as they can. We are not called to work for ourselves but to serve others. This is the opposite of what should be happening for God's people.

Even the church hoards money! That's how far the creation has fallen. Churches hoard millions of dollars instead of giving it to those who need it. This is an absolute violation of God's law, His heart, and the creation's intent.

Picture the church with a fund of five million dollars, sitting in investments while families in their own congregation struggle to pay rent. Picture the orphan without food or shelter, and the church claiming, "We need to be good stewards." So they hoard the money away to ensure their own financial security.

This is greed masquerading as wisdom. This is fear masquerading as prudence.

If all mankind is contaminated, then it stands to reason that all mankind within the church is contaminated. The people within the church do what this world does, and this is sin. The church has lost its saltiness. They take God's money, God's treasure, and invest it in this world for a greater return. They invest God's money into funds that propagate hate, greed, lust, and selfishness. These church leaders who hoard money, just as the world does, will be held accountable for what they've done with God's treasure.

What the Manual Says About Greed

Warnings Against Greed:

• "You shall not covet your neighbor's house... or anything that belongs to your neighbor." (Exodus 20:17)

• "The greedy stir up conflict, but those who trust in the Lord will prosper." (Proverbs 28:25)

• "Woe to him who piles up stolen goods and makes himself wealthy by extortion! How long must this go on?" (Habakkuk 2:6)

• "From the least to the greatest, all are greedy for gain; prophets and priests alike, all practice deceit." (Jeremiah 6:13)

• "Watch out! Be on your guard against all kinds of greed; life does not consist in an abundance of possessions." (Luke 12:15)

Consequences of Greed:

• "The greedy bring ruin to their households." (Proverbs 15:27)

• "A faithful man will abound with blessings, but whoever hastens to be rich will not go unpunished." (Proverbs 28:20)

- "In their greed these teachers will exploit you with fabricated stories. Their condemnation has long been hanging over them." (2 Peter 2:3)
- "Nor thieves nor the greedy nor drunkards nor slanderers nor swindlers will inherit the kingdom of God." (1 Corinthians 6:10)
- "Those who want to get rich fall into temptation and a trap... that plunge people into ruin and destruction." (1 Timothy 6:9)

Checklist to Combat Greed:

☐ "Better the little that the righteous have than the wealth of many wicked." (Psalm 37:16)

☐ "Keep your lives free from the love of money and be content with what you have, because God has said: 'Never will I leave you; never will I forsake you.'" (Hebrews 13:5)

☐ "Command those who are rich in this present world not to be arrogant nor to put their hope in wealth... but to put their hope in God." (1 Timothy 6:17)

☐ "Do not store up for yourselves treasures on earth, where moths and vermin destroy, and where thieves break in and steal. But store up for yourselves treasures in heaven." (Matthew 6:19 20)

☐ "No one can serve two masters... You cannot serve both God and money." (Matthew 6:24)

☐ "Put to death... greed, which is idolatry." (Colossians 3:5)

You must remember an important thing about combating greed: *the gift frees the giver*.

5. LUST
I Want It!

We often think of lust as just sexual desire. But that is a deception of the mind. Lust is the desire for things of this world. Anything, absolutely anything you desire of this world comes from lust.

That new phone that just came out? Lust. That vacation you scroll through on Instagram, feeling that pull in your chest? Lust. That person at work who isn't your spouse, who makes you feel seen and understood? Lust. The recognition you crave, the promotion you obsess over, the likes and comments you refresh your screen waiting for? All lust.

Lust corrupts the heart, distorts God's design, and leads to destruction. Unregulated desire enslaves the spirit. We are to seek after what is holy, not what is unholy.

If darkness can guide our mind to lust and desire after the objects of this world, then we lose sight of our purpose and what we were created for.

What the Manual Says About Lust

Warnings Against Lust:
- "The lust of the flesh, the lust of the eyes, and the pride of life, comes not from the Father but from the world." (1 John 2:16)
- "You shall not commit adultery. But I tell you that anyone who looks at a woman lustfully has already committed adultery with her in his heart." (Matthew 5:27 28)
- "The eye is the lamp of the body. If your eyes are healthy, your whole body will be full of light." (Matthew 6:22 23)
- "The acts of the flesh are obvious: sexual immorality, impurity and debauchery... those who live like this will not inherit the kingdom of God." (Galatians 5:19, 21)

Consequences of Lust:
- "For a prostitute can be had for a loaf of bread, but another man's wife preys on your very life." (Proverbs 6:26)
- "Can a man scoop fire into his lap without his clothes being burned?" (Proverbs 6:27)
- "After desire has conceived, it gives birth to sin; and sin, when it is full-grown, gives birth to death." (James 1:15)

Checklist to Combat Lust:

SELF-REGULATION

☐ "Flee from sexual immorality. All other sins a person commits are outside the body, but whoever sins sexually sins against their own body." (1 Corinthians 6:18)

☐ "Put to death, therefore, whatever belongs to your earthly nature: sexual immorality, impurity, lust, evil desires and greed, which is idolatry." (Colossians 3:5)

☐ "But among you there must not be even a hint of sexual immorality, or of any kind of impurity... because these are improper for God's holy people." (Ephesians 5:3)

☐ "Make a covenant with your eyes not to look lustfully at a young woman." (Job 31:1)

☐ "Blessed are the pure in heart, for they will see God." (Matthew 5:8)

Lust is a fire that consumes and destroys, but discipline preserves life and brings closeness to God. Regulating your desires, guarding your eyes, your heart, and your mind, is essential, because without self-control, lust can inflict deep and lasting damage.

But lust is only one form of desire that can lead us astray. There are other cravings, less obvious but just as powerful, which can steal our devotion and subtly shape our lives.

IDOLS: THE DECEPTION OF MODERN WORSHIP

We mock the ancient Israelites for melting down gold to craft a calf, bowing before it, and offering sacrifices. We think,

"How foolish. How could they worship something they made with their own hands?"

But this is the deception at work in your mind right now. You might think you are exempt, that because you do not bow to a golden statue, you are not worshiping idols.

L et me show you what you have not seen.

PART FIVE: THE THINGS YOU BOW TO

THOSE ANCIENT PEOPLE did not have what you have. They did not have the Internet, airplanes, or athletes with superhuman skill. They did not have movie stars, fast cars, or skyscrapers. The golden calf was the most magnificent thing they could create, a symbol of power, beauty, and human achievement.

So what is yours?

The Fascination of Flight

Why do people stop and stare when an airplane passes overhead? What is that pull in your chest when you see something soaring through the sky?

Why are there entire museums dedicated to airplanes? Buildings filled with these machines, polished and displayed like sacred relics. People travel from around the world to see them, to walk beneath them, to take photographs standing next to them.

And the pilots, have you noticed how they're treated? Walk through an airport in uniform and observe the reactions. People move aside. They stare. A child asks, "Are you a pilot?" and when the answer is yes, their eyes widen. "Wow, that's incredible."

Why is that?

What are you actually admiring? The machine? Or what the machine represents, human power, human achievement, human mastery over the natural world: Man flying.

This is idol worship. You just don't call it that.

The Idol of History

What about history? We have entire universities built around it. Departments dedicated to studying it. Museums were constructed to preserve it. We spend billions of dollars to maintain buildings where significant events occurred, to protect artifacts from the past, and to ensure that what humans have accomplished is never forgotten.

But what is history, really?

It is the admiration of human achievement. It is the reverence of what man has done, what man has built, what man has conquered. It looks backward at human accomplishment and says, "Humankind is incredible."

When you stand in a museum and marvel at what ancient civilizations built, what kings accomplished, what empires conquered, you are engaging in the same act as the Israelites bowing before the golden calf. You are reveling in the created things rather than the Creator.

SELF-REGULATION

"They exchanged the truth about God for a lie, and worshiped and served created things rather than the Creator..."
Romans 1:25

A dmiration of the past is reveling in the creation over the Creator.

The Deception of "We Don't Do That"

The whisper of pride says, "I don't worship idols. I'm not like those ancient people. I'm too smart for that. Too enlightened. Too modern."

But this is exactly what God was showing us through the Israelites. He was revealing what idol worship looks like so we could recognize it in ourselves. And what have we done? We've looked at their exact actions and said, "Well, I don't do *that specific thing*, so I must be free of it."

This is the deceit of the contaminated mind. It convinces you that because you don't perform the identical ritual, you don't have the identical problem.

You don't bow to a golden calf, so you think you're not an idolater.

But you do bow. You just bow differently.

You bow when you refresh your social media feed compulsively, seeking validation from the creation. You bow when you obsess over your career advancement, making an idol of your position and status. You bow when you arrange your entire life around your children's activities, making them the center of your worship instead of God.

You bow when you cannot miss a game, when you know every statistic of your favorite athlete, but can't name the fruits of the Spirit. You bow when you spend hours researching your next vacation, your next purchase, your next experience, pouring energy into created things that you should be pouring into knowing the Creator.

Sports: The Modern Temple

Look at a stadium. Tens of thousands gather in one place, at one time, unified in purpose. They wear the colors of their tribe. They chant together. They rise and fall together. They experience collective pleasure and collective despair.

They spend hundreds, sometimes thousands of dollars, for the privilege of being present. They plan their weeks, their months, their lives around the schedule of games. They teach their children the history, the legends, the sacred stories of their team.

What is this if not worship?

"But it's just entertainment," you say. "It's just fun. It's just something to enjoy."

Was the golden calf not entertainment? Was it not enjoyable to dance before it, to feast in its presence, to feel part of something larger than yourself?

The form changes. The heart remains the same. You are worshiping human achievement, the speed, the strength, the skill, the triumph of man. You are bowing before created things.

Celebrity: The Golden Image

We have created people whose faces are more recognizable than the face of Christ. We know their lives, their relationships, their struggles, their victories. We follow their every move. We defend them when they're criticized. We mourn when they fall.

We call them "icons." We say they're "legendary." We use the language of the sacred to honor the flesh.

And when they fail, when they're exposed as broken and contaminated like everyone else, we are devastated. Because we made them into something they were never meant to be. We made them into idols.

Technology: The New Altar

Your phone. How many times did you check it today? How many times did you feel that pull, that need to see what's happening, who's responded, what you're missing?

How much of your life is organized around it? How much of your identity is tied to it? How much of your sense of worth comes from it?

When was the last time you went a full day without it? Could you? Would you even want to?

This is not a tool you use. This is an altar you bow before. This is an idol that demands your constant attention, devotion, and sacrifice of time, presence, and peace. Because it serves the flesh, it gives you pleasure all the while contaminating you with the darkness of this world.

Money: The God We Serve

Jesus said, 'You cannot serve both God and money.' He didn't say it's difficult. He didn't say you probably shouldn't. He said you *cannot*. It's impossible.

But look at your life. Look at what you think about most. Look at what drives your decisions. Look at what you sacrifice for, what you stress over, what you hoard, what you trust for your security.

Is it God? Or is it the number in your bank account?

The Israelites thought the golden calf would provide for them, protect them, and guide them. You think your 401(k) will do the same. Different form. Same heart. Same idolatry.

Education: The Idol of Knowledge

We worship at the altar of degrees, credentials, and institutions. We trust in human wisdom more than divine truth. We spend years and fortunes pursuing knowledge of the creation while ignoring the wisdom of the Creator.

"I have a PhD," someone says, and the room grows quiet with reverence. The educated are treated as a priestly class, their words given weight and authority simply because they've been approved by an institution created by man.

B ut what does God say?

"The fear of the Lord is the beginning of knowledge, but fools despise wisdom and instruction." (Proverbs 1:7)

"See to it that no one takes you captive through hollow and deceptive philosophy, which depends on human tradition and the elemental spiritual forces of this world rather than on Christ." (Colossians 2:8)

The pursuit of knowledge is not wrong. But when it becomes the thing you worship, when your identity is tied to it, when you trust in it more than you trust in God, it has become an idol.

The Test of the Idol

How do you know if something is an idol in your life?

Ask yourself these questions:

- What do you think about most?
- What do you spend your money on?
- What do you spend your time on?
- What would devastate you if you lost it?
- What do you sacrifice for?
- What do you serve?

If the answer to any of these questions is anything other than God, you have an idol.

If losing your job would crush you more than losing our Father would, your job is an idol.

If you spend more time on your hobbies than in prayer and study of His Word, your hobbies are idols.

If you can't imagine life without your possessions but can easily imagine days without seeking God, your possessions are idols.

If you know more about your favorite team, your favorite show, your favorite celebrity than you know about the purpose of God, you are worshiping idols.

The Israelites weren't stupid. They were human. Just like you.

Breaking Free from Idols

Recognizing the idol is the first step. But recognition without action is worthless.

You must destroy the idol. Not physically, though sometimes that's necessary too, but spiritually. You must remove it from the throne of your heart, where only God belongs.

This will hurt. The idol has roots. It has given you comfort, identity, purpose, and pleasure. Removing it will feel like tearing out part of yourself.

But that's exactly what it is. The idol is not you. It's a contamination, a growth, a tumor that has attached itself to you and convinced you that you cannot live without it.

You can. You were designed to live with God alone at the center. Everything else is invasion, infection, idolatry.

What the Manual Says About Idolatry

Warnings Against Idolatry:

- "Do not make for yourselves an idol in the form of anything in heaven above or on the earth beneath or in the waters below." (Exodus 20:4)
- "Do not turn to idols or make metal gods for yourselves. I am the Lord your God." (Leviticus 19:4)
- "Those who cling to worthless idols turn away from God's love for them." (Jonah 2:8)
- "Dear children, keep yourselves from idols." (1 John 5:21)
- "They worshiped and served created things rather than

the Creator—who is forever praised." (Romans 1:25)

Consequences of Idolatry:

- "They followed worthless idols and became worthless themselves." (2 Kings 17:15)
- "Their land is full of idols; they bow down to the work of their hands." (Isaiah 2:8)
- "Because of this, God gave them over to shameful lusts." (Romans 1:26)
- "Outside are the dogs, those who practice magic arts, the sexually immoral, the murderers, the idolaters." (Revelation 22:15)
- "For of this you can be sure: no immoral, impure or greedy person—such a person is an idolater—has any inheritance in the kingdom of Christ and of God." (Ephesians 5:5)

Checklist to Overcome Idolatry:

☐ "Worship the Lord your God, and serve him only." (Matthew 4:10)

☐ "You shall have no other gods before me." (Exodus 20:3)

☐ "Set your minds on things above, not on earthly things." (Colossians 3:2)

☐ "Flee from idolatry." (1 Corinthians 10:14)

☐ "We know also that the Son of God has come and has given us understanding, so that we may know him who is true." (1 John 5:20)

☐ "Choose for yourselves this day whom you will serve... But as for me and my household, we will serve the Lord." (Joshua 24:15)

The golden calf is still here. It no longer resembles gold. It looks like success. It looks like comfort. It looks like entertainment. It looks like security. It looks like everything you've been taught to want, to work for, to desire.

But it's still an idol. And it will still destroy you if you bow before it.

PART SIX: PRACTICAL SELF-REGULATION

YOU'VE SEEN THE FIVE infections. You know their names, their tactics, their consequences. You have the checklists from the manual. But knowing is not enough. The gap between knowledge and action is where most people remain trapped their entire lives.

Solomon had all the wisdom in the world and still fell. The Pharisees knew every word of Scripture and still missed the Messiah. Knowledge without application is just noise in a contaminated mind.

So how do you bridge that gap? How do you move from understanding that you're infected to actually living differently?

This is where self-regulation becomes practical.

Recognizing the Good to Avoid the Bad

Self-regulation is recognizing the good that will help you avoid the bad and acting out of your own desire to avoid natural consequences. Taking measures to ensure our well-being is the very definition of love.

We are enslaved by the thoughts, the contamination, and the evil within our minds. But God takes what is evil and turns it into good, provided you choose it. For someone who does not force their mind to choose good when the option is available, will automatically choose the evil influence they feel.

This too is self-regulation: choosing what is good even when influenced by what is not.

Pleasure Is the Result of Sin

You may ask yourself, "But I feel good. This feels right."

But is it really good, or simply a pleasure?

Pleasure feels good, but only for a moment. You longed for that new car, and when you finally got it, you felt a rush of satisfaction. However, the excitement soon faded. The same is true with lust; the thrill is quick, but it is shallow, fleeting, and empty.

Make no mistake: sin does feel good. That is what makes it dangerous. Your feelings are corrupted, and they cannot be trusted to lead you into the truth.

Conviction, on the other hand, comes from the Spirit. It's that weight in your heart that tells you something is not right. The difference between conviction of the Spirit and the pleasure of sin is a fine line, which is why we cannot rely on emotion.

We must return to the manual. What does God's Word say? What aligns with it? That is why we have sixty-six books of guidance, because apart from them, it is impossible to discern truth from deception.

So, Can We Really Avoid Consequences?

So knowing that your mind is corrupted and that your mind is deceived, you must fight and do everything you can to come through this wall of darkness and find the light. Yes, the checklists are absolutely necessary to avoid the cruel consequences of this world. And can you actually avoid all of them? No. But you can minimize their impact on your life.

Normally, it's the natural consequences in this world that keep us within certain limits. But what if we could foresee those consequences and avoid them through self-regulation? Could we avoid suffering? Could we avoid more pain?

It is possible. This life wasn't meant to be free of suffering, so we will never be able to avoid it completely. But if we can learn through wisdom, self-discipline, and self-regulation, then we could minimize the impact of natural consequences.

However, you must first know what is right to avoid these natural consequences. You must know what is correct. This is an absolute truth, and this is unavoidable.

Y ou must know the correct course of action to avoid the wrong course of action.

T his is the first step in self-regulation.

The Real Purpose of This Life

Whether you know it or not, darkness exists. In fact, you would have to be blind and deaf and stick your head in a hole in the ground to not know that evil exists. It is so prevalent in this world that all you have to do is turn on the TV or look at social media to see it at work.

So how do you avoid evil? How do you avoid the consequences associated with it?

First, you must become aware that there are consequences of evil. If you cannot see the consequences, then you cannot avoid them. And even if you can see them, they are very hard to avoid.

This is not about making your life here easier. I apologize for disappointing you.

This is about preparing you for eternal life. This is for the ones who fight, the ones who desire to truly live. This place here is merely temporary. The importance of what we call life here is in what it can produce for us.

Can it produce a loving spirit? A spirit of kindness? Can it produce a life of giving? Can what we do here produce the fruit that God desires within us?

Self-regulation is about shaping the spirit within, rather than feeding the desires of the flesh.

Can you get out of bed, go to work, and push through the hate that feels so heavy? Are you able to release the power of greed over your life through an act of giving? Can you power through the clinginess of selfishness to share what God has given you?

This is the self-regulation that gives life, that breathes love into an eternal spirit.

But understanding what self-regulation is and actually doing it are two different things. You can know every verse in the manual and still live as a slave to the whispers. The real test comes not in the reading, but in the walking.

And the path you must walk goes directly through darkness.

PART SEVEN: PATH THROUGH DARKNESS

WE MUST WALK THROUGH FIRE

We will walk through trials. We will walk through fire, and we will be refined because of it. When you are contaminated with evil, there is no other option. We must push forward and fight against all this evil. We have to walk through the valley of the shadow of death in order to get to the promise of a life with no evil.

Evil kills, deceives, lies, robs, abuses, betrays, hoards, boasts, desires, and destroys everything that it can. But we are here not only to recognize the contamination of the mind and to self-regulate to minimize its consequences, but also to illuminate a path forward.

There Is No Easy Way

Let me be clear about what this path demands.

You will lose things. Relationships that were built on shared contamination will fall apart when you choose differently. Jobs that require you to operate in greed or hate will become unbearable. Comforts you relied on will reveal themselves as chains.

You will be misunderstood.

When you choose what is good in a world that rewards compromise, your very presence becomes a form of confrontation. Those who cling to what is corrupt will see your refusal as judgment, your integrity as arrogance, your love as rejection. They will not understand that goodness exposes what prefers to remain hidden.

To choose the light is to walk a path against the world. Those around you will feel the weight of their own guilt in your presence. They will grow uneasy, not because you condemn them, but because the good reflected in your life reveals what they've hidden in theirs.

L ight exposes darkness, and few are ready to see what lives in the shadows.

Y ou will fail. Not once, not occasionally, but repeatedly. You'll check the checklist one day and ignore it the next. You'll recognize hate and choose it anyway. You'll see fear paralyzing you and still refuse to move.

This is not a clean path. This is not a three-step program. This is walking through fire with the promise that what survives will be pure.

Why the Darkness Is Necessary

But here's what you must understand: the darkness is not punishment. The darkness is revelation.

Every time you feel hate rising and choose love anyway, you learn what love costs. Every time fear whispers and you move forward despite it, you discover what courage actually is. Every time greed tightens its grip and you give anyway, you experience what freedom feels like.

The contamination cannot be cleansed by understanding it. It can only be burned away in the fires of courage, by walking the path that exposes it, resists it, and destroys it.

This is why there are no shortcuts. This is why knowledge alone cannot save anyone. This is why the checklist exists; however, following it requires walking through the valley.

The Dawn Beyond the Night

This path forward, the path through the darkness, is what we look to for hope. Because without hope, there is no purpose in life, and you have been given a purpose.

So what is that purpose? What lies at the end of this path through fire and shadow? What remains when all the contamination is burned away?

The answer has been in front of you this entire time.

PART EIGHT: THE ANSWER IS LOVE

WHAT REMAINS WHEN DARKNESS Is Removed

If you were to remove all of the darkness, all of the hate, fear, greed, selfishness, and lust, what you would end up with is purity, love.

We were created in love, from love, and for love. But what you see now with your eyes, what you are able to feel, touch, and hear, is the contamination of that love. It is what happens when darkness is mixed with the light.

Love Is the Foundation

Love is the foundation of our existence. It is the fulfillment of God's will. Without love, all acts of service, sacrifice, and faith mean nothing. Love is not optional; it is the life source that feeds us all and guides us to eternity.

The Call to Love

- "Love the Lord your God with all your heart and with all your soul and with all your mind." (Matthew 22:37)
- "Love your neighbor as yourself." (Matthew 22:39)
- "By this everyone will know that you are my disciples, if you love one another." (John 13:35)
- "Above all, love each other deeply, because love covers over a multitude of sins." (1 Peter 4:8)
- "Let all that you do be done in love." (1 Corinthians 16:14)

The Nature of Love

- "This is love: not that we loved God, but that he loved us and sent his Son as an atoning sacrifice for our sins." (1 John 4:10)
- "Greater love has no one than this: to lay down one's life for one's friends." (John 15:13)
- "Hate evil, love good; maintain justice in the courts." (Amos 5:15)
- "Do everything in love." (1 Corinthians 16:14)

The Power of Love

- "Love does no harm to a neighbor. Therefore love is the fulfillment of the law." (Romans 13:10)
- "God is love. Whoever lives in love lives in God, and God in them." (1 John 4:16)
- "Many waters cannot quench love; rivers cannot sweep it away." (Song of Solomon 8:7)
- "Over all these virtues put on love, which binds them all together in perfect unity." (Colossians 3:14)
- "Three things will last forever, faith, hope, and love, and the greatest of these is love." (1 Corinthians 13:13)

First Corinthians 13:4-8

SELF-REGULATION

Love is patient, love is kind. It does not envy, it does not boast, it is not proud. It does not dishonor others, it is not self-seeking, it is not easily angered, it keeps no record of wrongs. Love does not delight in evil but rejoices with the truth. It always protects, always trusts, always hopes, always perseveres. Love never fails.

L ook at this passage carefully. Look at what love is NOT:
- Not envious (combats greed)
- Not boastful or proud (combats pride)
- Not self-seeking (combats selfishness)
- Not easily angered (combats hate)

Love is the antidote to every infection. Love is what remains when you strip away the contamination. Love is your original design, your true nature before darkness entered the light.

But love doesn't exist in isolation. Love that stays hidden in the heart, that never manifests in the world, is incomplete. This is why we must talk about the outward expression of what burns within.

PART NINE: KINDNESS AND EXPRESSION

WE CANNOT FORGET KINDNESS

Kindness is the outward expression of love, reflecting the mercy and gentleness of God. It softens hearts, heals wounds, and overcomes evil with good. We are commanded to clothe ourselves in kindness, for it is the mark of His character.

Where love is the internal reality, kindness is the external manifestation. You cannot have one without the other. Love without kindness is not love, it's deceit.

Real love shows up in the small moments: patience with the cashier, respect for the waiter, compassion for the stranger. Anyone can say "I love people," but if that love doesn't translate into gentleness, respect, and care for those around us, it's not love. It's deception. For you will know the tree by the fruit it produces.

The Call to Kindness

• "Be kind and compassionate to one another, forgiving each other, just as in Christ God forgave you." (Ephesians 4:32)

- "Therefore, as God's chosen people, holy and dearly loved, clothe yourselves with compassion, kindness, humility, gentleness and patience." (Colossians 3:12)

- "Love your enemies, do good to them, and lend to them without expecting to get anything back." (Luke 6:35)

- "A man who is kind benefits himself, but a cruel man hurts himself." (Proverbs 11:17)

- "Do not neglect to show hospitality to strangers, for thereby some have entertained angels unawares." (Hebrews 13:2)

The Nature of Kindness

- "The Lord is righteous in all his ways and kind in all his works." (Psalm 145:17)

- "But when the kindness and love of God our Savior appeared, he saved us..." (Titus 3:4–5)

- "Love is patient, love is kind." (1 Corinthians 13:4)

- "A gentle answer turns away wrath, but a harsh word stirs up anger." (Proverbs 15:1)

- "The fruit of the Spirit is love, joy, peace, forbearance, kindness, goodness, faithfulness..." (Galatians 5:22)

The Power of Kindness

- "Your kindness will reward you, but your cruelty will destroy you." (Proverbs 11:17)

- "Do not be overcome by evil, but overcome evil with good." (Romans 12:21)

SELF-REGULATION

- "If your enemy is hungry, give him bread to eat, and if he is thirsty, give him water to drink." (Proverbs 25:21)
- "In everything, set them an example by doing what is good." (Titus 2:7)
- "Blessed are the merciful, for they will be shown mercy." (Matthew 5:7)

CONCLUSION: THE FIGHT FOR LOVE

THIS IS THE BATTLE

You now understand the contamination. You now see the five principal infections: hate, fear, pride, greed, and lust. You now know they work together, feeding off each other, multiplying through your thoughts into actions that bring natural consequences.

You now understand the manual, the 66 books that serve as your checklist, your standard operating procedures for life on Earth.

You now understand that self-regulation is not about making your life here comfortable. It is about shaping your spirit for eternity. It is about recognizing the whispers before they become actions, and choosing good when every influence screams for you to choose evil.

The Simple Truth

The airline industry learned through tragedy that minds fail. So they built checklists. Corporations learned that people disagree on what's right. So they built policy manuals. And God, who has always known that our minds are contaminated, gave us the Bible.

The question is: will you use it?

Will you recognize that your irritation at the slow driver is hate whispering? Will you acknowledge that your reluctance to give is a combination of greed and fear? Will you see that your need to be right is pride blinding you? Will you admit that your desire for that person, that thing, that object is lust enslaving you?

Self-Regulation in Practice
Self-regulation means:
- Being humble even though pride says you know more
- Giving away money even though fear and greed scream to hold on
- Speaking kindly even though hate wants to criticize
- Taking action for good even though fear paralyzes
- Pursuing holiness even though lust pulls toward the world

Self-regulation means making decisions before the whispers control your thoughts. It means creating systems that compensate for your contaminated mind. It means following the checklist even when you don't feel like it.

The Purpose That Was Hidden

Your purpose has been hidden from you by the contamination of the mind, but I am revealing it to you now:

Your purpose is love.

N ot the feeling of love. Not the sentiment of love. But the active, sacrificial, patient, kind, non-envious, non-boastful, non-proud, non-self-seeking, not-easily-angered, keeps-no-record-of-wrongs, does-not-delight-in-evil, rejoices-with-truth, always-protects, always-trusts, always-hopes, always-perseveres kind of love.

The love that costs you something. The love that gives when greed says take. The love that speaks truth when fear says be silent. The love that serves when pride says you deserve to be served. The love that remains faithful when lust says to wander.

This Is Not Easy

I will not lie to you and tell you this is easy. You will fail. You will give in to the whispers. You will forget to check the checklist. You will act on impulse instead of principle. You will be contaminated again and again and again.

But that is why we have the manual. That is why we have self-regulation. That is why we fight.

Because every time you recognize hate and choose love instead, you are being refined. Every time you feel fear and step forward anyway, you are being shaped. Every time you choose to give instead of hoard, you are becoming who you were created to be.

The Valley of the Shadow

We must walk through the valley of the shadow of death to get to the promise of a life with no evil. There is no way around it. The contamination is too deep. The darkness is too pervasive. The only way out is through.

But you do not walk alone. The One who gave you the manual walks with you. The One who gave you the checklist created the list from His own character. The One who calls you to love is love.

The Final Word

Self-regulation is not the destination. Love is the destination.

Self-regulation is the tool that gets you there, the daily practice of recognizing contamination and choosing purity, of hearing the whispers and rejecting them, of following the checklist even when your mind screams that you know better.

But here is what I need you to understand: you were not created for struggle. You were created for love. Every battle you fight against hate, every moment you resist fear, every time you choose humility over pride, every act of giving that breaks greed's hold, every pursuit of purity over lust, all of it is simply clearing away the rubble to reveal what was always underneath.

YOU.

The you that God made. The you who loves without counting the cost. The you who gives without measuring the return. The you who stands in the fire and does not burn because love is the fire, and you were made from it.

This guide is not meant to sit on a shelf gathering dust while you continue living as you always have. Return to it when hate whispers in your ear. Lean on it when fear paralyzes your feet. Let it show you what you cannot see, the contaminations so subtle, so normalized, that you've mistaken them for your own personality.

A nd never, ever forget this truth: *the gift frees the giver.*

W hen you give love, hate loses its grip on you. When you give trust, fear's chains fall away. When you give with humility, pride is extinguished. When you give generously, greed's fist unclenches. When you give light, lust's fire goes cold.

This is not a metaphor. This is a mechanism. This is how you are freed.

This is the fight, not for comfort, not for ease, not for a better life here. This is the fight for your spirit. This is the path through the valley of the shadow of death. This is the way home.

The checklist is not a burden. It is mercy. The manual is not restriction. It is grace. The standard operating procedures are not rules to trap you; they are the light of His presence guiding you through a darkness so thick you cannot see your own hand in front of your face.

One day, and that day will come, your eyes will close for the last time in this contaminated place. You will stand before Him, the Giver of every good gift, the One who held nothing back, who gave everything, who is love itself.

In that moment, only one question will matter:

Did you give as He gave? Did you love as He loved?

Not perfectly. You will never love perfectly here. But did you fight? Did you recognize the contamination and choose differently? Did you follow the checklist even when it cost you everything? Did you give when greed screamed to take? Did you love when hate felt so much easier?

The manual is in your hands. The choice is before you. It has always been before you, in every moment, in every decision, in every thought you chose to reject or accept.

Choose love. Choose life. Choose Him.

Because in the end, when all the darkness is burned away, love is all that remains. Love is all that was ever real. Love is what you were made from, made for, made to become.

And love never fails.

SELF-REGULATION

"Three things will last forever, faith, hope, and love, and the greatest of these is love." (1 Corinthians 13:13)

Also by Justin Boynton

- Your Deficiency Beliefs
- Tus Creencias de Deficiencia
- The Final Truth
- La Verdad Final
- The Final Report
- El Informe Final
- Self-Regulation
- Auto-Regulación